THE TRUTH ABOUT ME

Written by: Nykki L. Matthews
Illustrated by: HH-Pax

ISBN: 978-1-7360727-1-4 (Paperback)
ISBN: 978-1-7360727-0-7 (Hardcover)

Any references to historical events, real people, or real places are used fictitiously. Names, characters, and places are products of the author's imagination.

Illustrator: Book design by HH-PAX

Printed in the United States of America.

First printing edition 2021.

Mylestones & Co.
1335 Jefferson Road
P.O. Box 22684
Rochester, New York 14692
www.mylestonesandco.com

Dedication:

When I finally mustered up the courage to show my 6-year-old son the final sketch of the main character, Jody, this was our conversation:

> Me: Myles, what do you think about this kid?
> Myles: I like him.
> Me: What do you like about him?
> Myles: He has skin like me?
> Me: (close to tears) – OK, buddy.

May all the other boys and girls who don't see main characters with skin like theirs enjoy this book. May you, too, muster up the courage to create and move into spaces where there aren't many with skin like yours and shift the narratives.

May my boys, always know that I will fight for them.
May my husband always know that I'll care for him.
May James, always know that he is missed.
For all the support and love throughout this journey - thank you!
God bless.

This Book Belongs To

First Name

_____
Last Name

Hi, my name is Jody. My truth is mine and I am sharing it with you.

The truth about me is that I love to investigate
problems and look for a solution.

The truth about me is that I am caring and honest.

The truth about me is that I love an adventurous trip.
My favorite means of transportation is by plane.

The truth about me is that I love school, and learning about history.

The truth about me is that I love my friends.

The truth about me is that I'm perfect as I am.

The truth about me is that my hair can be coiled, straight or curly and that's perfectly perfect!

The truth about me is that my skin is rich and beautiful, just like the history of my ancestors.

The truth about me is that breakfast
is my favorite meal of the day.

The truth about me is that,
when I run I feel free.

The truth about me is that I love
music, instruments and math.

The truth is that I love being with my family because they remind me of my truth.

My truth is mine. What's yours?

MY TRUTH IS MINE.
WHAT'S YOURS?

Write 4 Truths about yourself.

1. My Truth is that I _____

_____

_____

_____

2. My Truth is that I _____

_____

_____

_____

MY TRUTH IS MINE.
WHAT'S YOURS?

3. My Truth is that I _____

_____

_____

_____

4. My Truth is that I _____

_____

_____

_____

About the Author – Nykki L. Matthews

Nykki Matthews loves writing almost as much as she adores children. An 80's baby born in Florida and raised in New York, her superpowers are listening and building relationships. As a defender of children, it is in her heart to create a children's series that encourages and uplifts black and brown boys and girls. She believes that penning these stories will reflect the richness, gentleness, care, and depth of love within our communities.

As an educator, counselor, coach, and mentor, Nykki enjoys listening to children and hearing their perspectives on various topics. Delightfully ordinary and strong, she's afforded the best view and learns daily from her three beautiful and kind boys, Myles, Christian, and Wells. Nykki resides in New York with her thoughtful and dedicated husband, Tori, and together they are creating a legacy for generations to come.

Nykki's postsecondary education has afforded her the opportunity to merge the best classroom practices with her passion for education. She earned a Master of Science in School Counseling from the University of Rochester's Warner School of Education, a Bachelor of Science from Buffalo State College in Sociology and an Associate Degree from Monroe Community College in Liberal Arts with a concentration in education.

When not writing and caring for her family, Nykki also enjoys listening to music, quietness and car rides with her family.